GEOGRAPHY

*At press time, the situation in the Soviet Union was so fluid that information may no longer be accurate. Future editions of the book will reflect subsequent developments.

SIMON & SCHUSTER BOOKS FOR YOUNG READERS
Simon & Schuster Building, Rockefeller Center
1230 Avenue of the Americas, New York, New York 10020
Copyright © 1991 by Grisewood & Dempsey Ltd.
First U.S. edition 1992
All rights reserved including the right of reproduction
in whole or in part in any form.
Originally published in Great Britain by Grisewood & Dempsey Ltd.
SIMON & SCHUSTER BOOKS FOR YOUNG READERS
is a trademark of Simon & Schuster.
Series editor: Jackie Gaff
Editor: Sue Nicholson
Consultant: Keith Lye
Series designer: Ben White Associates
Illustrations by: Julie Carpenter (pp. 40-1, 52-3), Chris Forsey
(pp. 23, 28-9, 37, 56-7, 59, 60, 63, 83, 35, 37) Hayward Art Group
(pp. 42-3, 54-5, 68-9, 30-1, 90-1), Kevin Maddison (pp. 24-5, 38-9, 50-1,
66-7, 78-9, 88-9), Alex Pang (pp. 6, 8-9, 26-7, 64-5),
Swanston Graphics Limited (pp. 4-5, 7, 10-19, 30-3, 44-7, 58, 61, 70-3, 82-5).
Flags: Alan Cooper, à la carte

Manufactured in Hong Kong.

10 9 8 7 6 5 4 3 2 1   (pbk) 10 9 8 7 6 5 4 3 2

Library of Congress Cataloging-in-Publication Data
Bender, Lionel. Picture pocket : geography / by Lionel Bender.
p.   cm.   Includes index. Summary: Includes maps with text which present
information about the rivers, mountains, deserts, cities,
and countries on each of the six continents.
1. Geography—Juvenile literature.   [1. Atlases.   2. Geography.]   I. Title.
G133.B46   1992   910—dc20   91-29406   CIP
ISBN: 0-671-75996-5   ISBN: 0-671-75997-3

GEOGRAPHY

LIONEL BENDER

SIMON & SCHUSTER BOOKS FOR YOUNG READERS
Published by Simon & Schuster
New York   London   Toronto   Sydney   Tokyo   Singapore

CONTENTS

MAPPING THE WORLD

Maps are drawings of the Earth's surface as if seen from above. They show the shape of the land and the sea. They can also show the position of rivers, lakes, and cities and the height of the land. Because the Earth is shaped like a ball with a slightly flattened top and bottom, the most accurate map is a globe – a round model of the world.

When we turn a globe we can see the different parts of the Earth's surface, as shown below. The lines running across and down the globe are called lines of latitude and longitude. They help us to find places on a map. The line of latitude running around the Earth's middle is called the Equator.

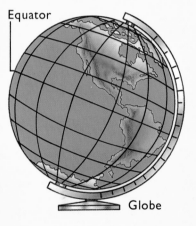

Equator

Globe

Most maps, though, are projections, or flat drawings of pieces of the globe. It is impossible to make a curved surface flat without twisting some pieces. Try drawing a picture on the outside of an orange. Now peel the orange and flatten out the peel on a table. What has happened to your drawing? In the same way, all map projections of the Earth's surface are distorted, or twisted out of shape.

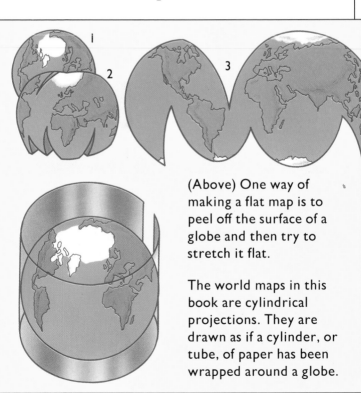

(Above) One way of making a flat map is to peel off the surface of a globe and then try to stretch it flat.

The world maps in this book are cylindrical projections. They are drawn as if a cylinder, or tube, of paper has been wrapped around a globe.

Guide to the Maps

In this book, there are relief maps and political maps. The relief maps show rivers, mountains, and deserts. They tell you about the physical features of the land. The political maps name the world's independent countries and their capital cities. Look at the key on the right to find out the meaning of the colors and symbols on these maps. The climate map on page 12 is different. It has a special key to tell you what the colors mean.

THE SUN'S RAYS

The Sun is the Earth's nearest star. It gives us heat and light which are vital to all life. The Sun's rays travel through the atmosphere, or layers of air, surrounding the Earth. At the poles, the rays are spread over a wider area, so the polar lands are always cold and icy. At the Equator, the Sun's rays are more intense. The hottest parts of the world are between the lines of latitude called the Tropics of Cancer and Capricorn.

Polar lands

Desert lands

KEY TO MAPS

⌇ River	⌒ Country boundary
◗ Lake	■ Capital city

Grassland

Dry grassland

Desert

Cool treeless area

Mountains

An independent country has its own border and flag, and its people control their own affairs. But some countries are not independent. For example, Greenland is controlled by Denmark and has Danish laws.

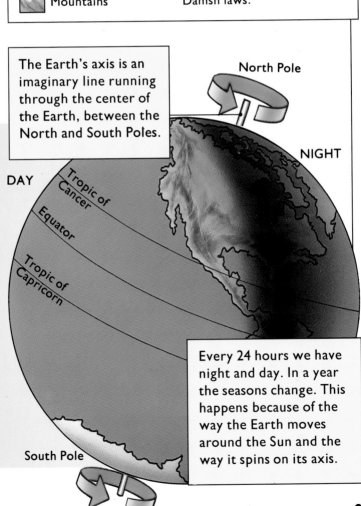

The Earth's axis is an imaginary line running through the center of the Earth, between the North and South Poles.

North Pole

NIGHT

DAY

Tropic of Cancer

Equator

Tropic of Capricorn

South Pole

Every 24 hours we have night and day. In a year the seasons change. This happens because of the way the Earth moves around the Sun and the way it spins on its axis.

Our Continents

The Earth's surface is covered by huge areas of water (our oceans and seas) and of land (our continents). There are seven continents: Africa, Antarctica, Asia, Australia, Europe, North America and South America. Some people say that because Europe and Asia are joined they make one big continent – Eurasia.

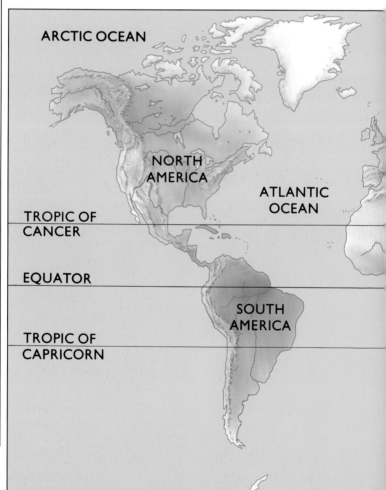

In this book we have divided the world into six main areas: Europe, Asia, North America, South America, Africa, and Oceania. Oceania is the name given to Australia, New Zealand, and the group of islands in the Pacific Ocean. The USSR*, the world's largest country, is in both Europe and Asia (see page 28).

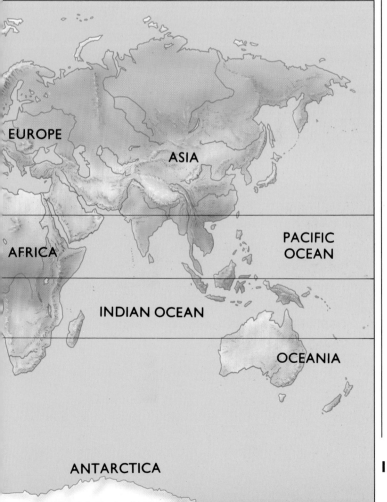

EUROPE

ASIA

AFRICA

PACIFIC OCEAN

INDIAN OCEAN

OCEANIA

ANTARCTICA

The Earth's Climates

Weather changes every day but "climate" describes the pattern of weather in an area over a long period of time. We say that one region is usually hot and wet and another is cool and dry. This depends on how far it is from the Equator and the sea. So Norway has a cool and rainy climate while Iran is hot and dry.

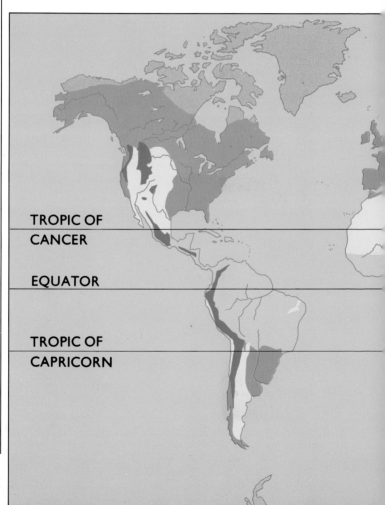

TROPIC OF
CANCER

EQUATOR

TROPIC OF
CAPRICORN

This key is for the climate map below. Polar lands are cold and icy all year round. You can read more about them on the next page. A temperate climate is mild and can be wet or dry. Areas near the Equator are hot and usually have plenty of rain every day.

CLIMATE KEY

Polar

Cool and snowy

Temperate

Dry land and desert

Tropical

Mountain

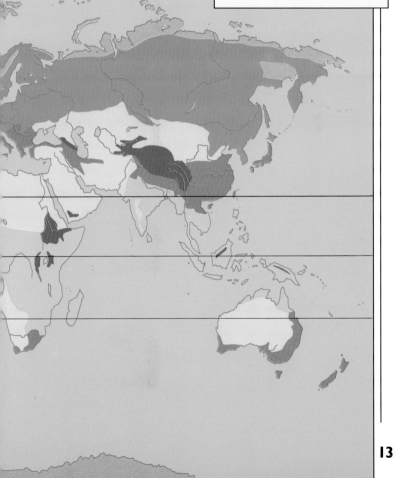

Polar Lands

The Arctic in the north and Antarctica in the south are the polar lands. We call their centers the North Pole and the South Pole. Antarctica is the world's fifth largest continent. It contains more than nine-tenths of the world's ice and snow and is the coldest place on Earth.

The Arctic is a large, mostly frozen ocean surrounded by islands. The Arctic Ocean is rich in wildlife.

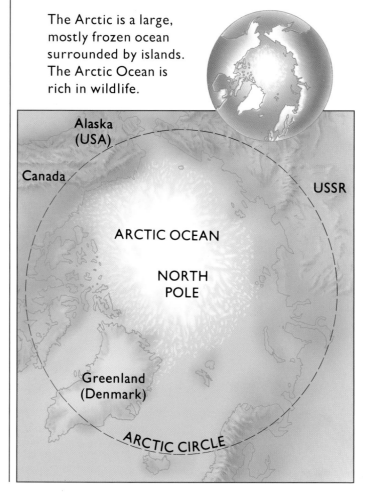

Alaska (USA)

Canada

USSR

ARCTIC OCEAN

NORTH POLE

Greenland (Denmark)

ARCTIC CIRCLE

In the icy polar lands the temperature is mostly below the freezing point, or 32°F, and it can fall to –58°F or more. In summer (May to August in the Arctic and November to February in Antarctica) the Sun never sets and some of the ice melts. In winter it is dark all day.

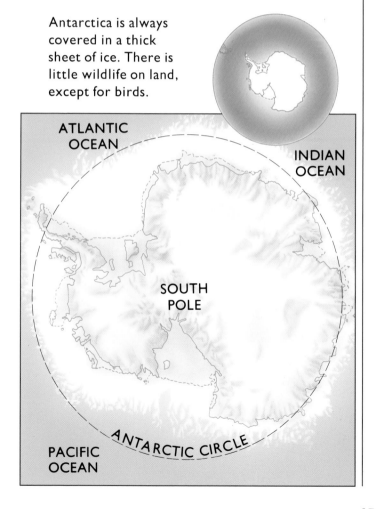

Antarctica is always covered in a thick sheet of ice. There is little wildlife on land, except for birds.

ATLANTIC
OCEAN

INDIAN
OCEAN

SOUTH
POLE

ANTARCTIC CIRCLE

PACIFIC
OCEAN

EUROPE

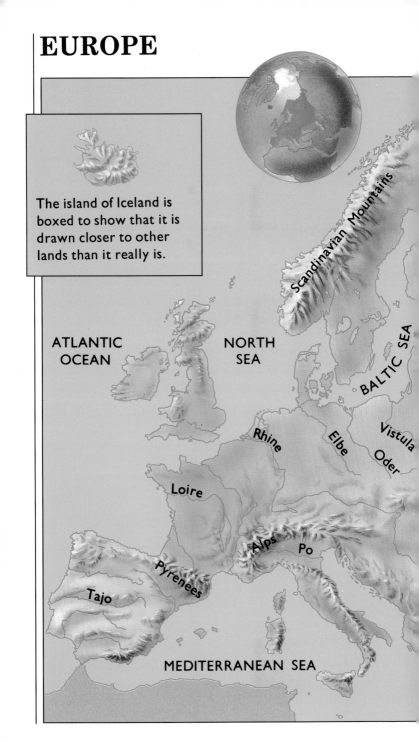

The island of Iceland is boxed to show that it is drawn closer to other lands than it really is.

Scandinavian Mountains

ATLANTIC OCEAN

NORTH SEA

BALTIC SEA

Rhine

Elbe

Vistula

Oder

Loire

Alps

Po

Pyrenees

Tajo

MEDITERRANEAN SEA

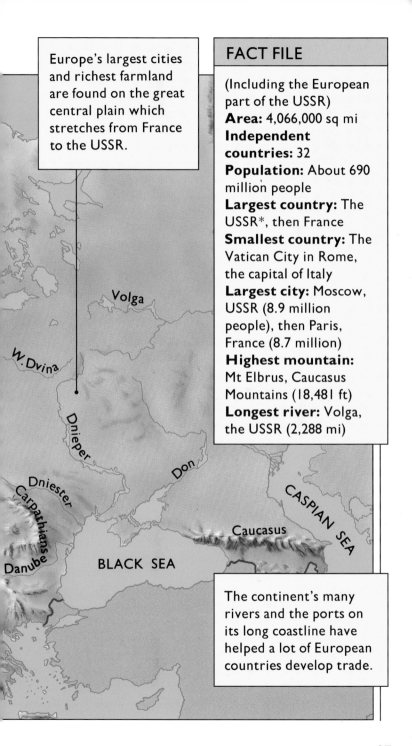

Europe's largest cities and richest farmland are found on the great central plain which stretches from France to the USSR.

FACT FILE

(Including the European part of the USSR)
Area: 4,066,000 sq mi
Independent countries: 32
Population: About 690 million people
Largest country: The USSR*, then France
Smallest country: The Vatican City in Rome, the capital of Italy
Largest city: Moscow, USSR (8.9 million people), then Paris, France (8.7 million)
Highest mountain: Mt Elbrus, Caucasus Mountains (18,481 ft)
Longest river: Volga, the USSR (2,288 mi)

Volga

W. Dvina

Dnieper

Dniester

Carpathians

Danube

Don

Caucasus

CASPIAN SEA

BLACK SEA

The continent's many rivers and the ports on its long coastline have helped a lot of European countries develop trade.

Countries and Capitals

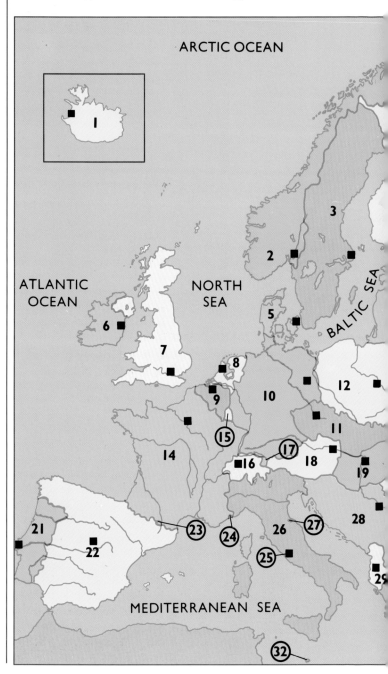

ARCTIC OCEAN

ATLANTIC OCEAN

NORTH SEA

BALTIC SEA

MEDITERRANEAN SEA

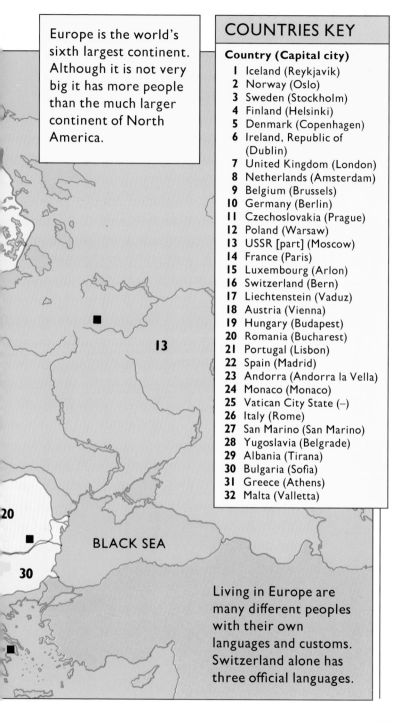

Europe is the world's sixth largest continent. Although it is not very big it has more people than the much larger continent of North America.

COUNTRIES KEY

Country (Capital city)

1 Iceland (Reykjavík)
2 Norway (Oslo)
3 Sweden (Stockholm)
4 Finland (Helsinki)
5 Denmark (Copenhagen)
6 Ireland, Republic of (Dublin)
7 United Kingdom (London)
8 Netherlands (Amsterdam)
9 Belgium (Brussels)
10 Germany (Berlin)
11 Czechoslovakia (Prague)
12 Poland (Warsaw)
13 USSR [part] (Moscow)
14 France (Paris)
15 Luxembourg (Arlon)
16 Switzerland (Bern)
17 Liechtenstein (Vaduz)
18 Austria (Vienna)
19 Hungary (Budapest)
20 Romania (Bucharest)
21 Portugal (Lisbon)
22 Spain (Madrid)
23 Andorra (Andorra la Vella)
24 Monaco (Monaco)
25 Vatican City State (–)
26 Italy (Rome)
27 San Marino (San Marino)
28 Yugoslavia (Belgrade)
29 Albania (Tirana)
30 Bulgaria (Sofia)
31 Greece (Athens)
32 Malta (Valletta)

13

20

BLACK SEA

30

Living in Europe are many different peoples with their own languages and customs. Switzerland alone has three official languages.

Facts and Figures

Country	Population	Official Language	Currency	Flag
1 Iceland	250,000	Icelandic	Krona	
2 Norway	4,240,000	Norwegian	Krone	
3 Sweden	8,580,000	Swedish	Swedish krona	
4 Finland	4,980,000	Finnish, Swedish	Markka	
5 Denmark	5,130,000	Danish	Krone	
6 Ireland, Republic of	3,500,000	English, Irish	Irish pound (punt)	
7 United Kingdom	57,240,000	English	Sterling pound	
8 Netherlands	14,910,000	Dutch	Guilder	
9 Belgium	9,930,000	Dutch, French	Belgian franc	

Country	Population	Official Language	Currency	Flag
10 Germany	78,620,000	German	Mark	
11 Czecho-slovakia	15,680,000	Czech, Slovak	Koruna	
12 Poland	37,930,000	Polish	Zloty	
13 USSR*	220,000,000 (Total – 290,000,000)	Russian	Rouble	
14 France	56,560,000	French	French franc	
15 Luxem-bourg	380,000	French, German	Arlon franc	
16 Switzer-land	6,650,000	French, German, Italian	Swiss franc	
17 Liechten-stein	28,000	German	Swiss franc	
18 Austria	7,660,000	German	Schilling	

Facts and Figures

Country	Population	Official Language	Currency	Flag
19 Hungary	10,550,000	Hungarian	Forint	
20 Romania	23,250,000	Romanian	Leu	
21 Portugal	10,470,000	Portuguese	Escudo	
22 Spain	39,330,000	Spanish	Peseta	
23 Andorra	50,000	Catalan	French franc, Spanish pesata	
24 Monaco	28,000	French	French franc	
25 Vatican City State	1,000	Italian, Latin	Italian lira	
26 Italy	57,640,000	Italian	Lira	
27 San Marino	23,000	Italian	Italian lira	

Country	Population	Official Language	Currency	Flag
28 Yugo-slavia	23,790,000	Serbo-Croatian, Slovene, Macedonian	Dinar	
29 Albania	3,200,000	Albanian	Lek	
30 Bulgaria	9,000,000	Bulgarian	Lev	
31 Greece	10,040,000	Greek	Drachma	
32 Malta	350,000	Maltese, English	Maltese pound	

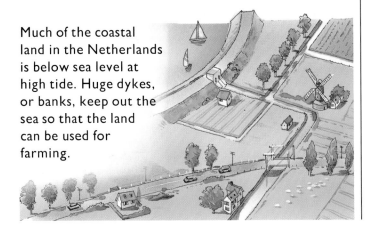

Much of the coastal land in the Netherlands is below sea level at high tide. Huge dykes, or banks, keep out the sea so that the land can be used for farming.

Sunny and Snowy Lands

Countries in the south of Europe near the Mediterranean Sea are called the Mediterranean countries. These sunny lands usually have hot, dry summers and mild, wet winters.

The northern countries of Iceland, Norway, Sweden, and Denmark are called Scandinavia. Scandinavia and Finland are cold and rainy with plenty of snow in the winter. Iceland and Norway have large fishing fleets.

Many people spend their vacations near the hot, sunny beaches of Greece and southern Spain.

In Italy, Greece, and southern Spain, farmers grow oranges, olives, and grapes for wine.

LAND OF THE MIDNIGHT SUN

The area in Scandinavia inside the Arctic Circle is sometimes called the "Land of the Midnight Sun" because at midsummer the Sun does not set. In winter it is dark 24 hours a day.

Hundreds of steep-sided valleys called fiords cut into Norway's rocky coastline, providing shelter for ships.

Winters are very cold in the far north of Europe so most people live near the sea, where the climate is a little warmer.

Farming and Industry

Europe has plenty of rich farmland. France, Germany, and the United Kingdom are three of the main farming countries. They are also among the world's major producers of iron and steel, electrical goods, and cars.

In the far north and in the eastern countries, thick forests are used for wood and for paper products. Many European countries have fishing fleets that harvest the rich waters along the rugged coastline.

Europe's main crops are wheat, oats, and barley. In some areas farmers grow sugar beet and potatoes.

Europe's many vine-yards and orchards are famous for their fine wines and fruit.

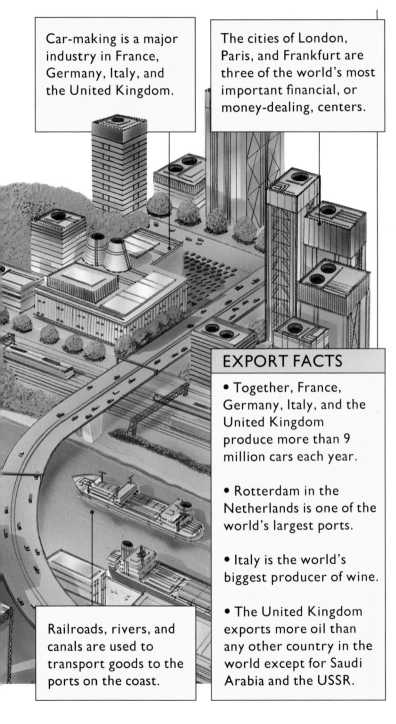

Car-making is a major industry in France, Germany, Italy, and the United Kingdom.

The cities of London, Paris, and Frankfurt are three of the world's most important financial, or money-dealing, centers.

EXPORT FACTS

• Together, France, Germany, Italy, and the United Kingdom produce more than 9 million cars each year.

• Rotterdam in the Netherlands is one of the world's largest ports.

• Italy is the world's biggest producer of wine.

• The United Kingdom exports more oil than any other country in the world except for Saudi Arabia and the USSR.

Railroads, rivers, and canals are used to transport goods to the ports on the coast.

The Biggest Country

The Union of Soviet Socialist Republics – the USSR* – is the world's largest country. It covers about one-sixth of the Earth's land area and stretches across both Europe and Asia.

Almost three-quarters of the USSR's 290 million people live in the European part of the country, west of the Ural Mountains. This region has plenty of farms and many large cities, including Moscow, the capital, and Leningrad.

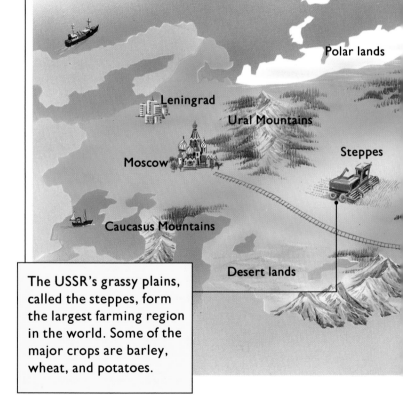

Polar lands

Leningrad

Ural Mountains

Steppes

Moscow

Caucasus Mountains

Desert lands

The USSR's grassy plains, called the steppes, form the largest farming region in the world. Some of the major crops are barley, wheat, and potatoes.

28

OFFICIAL LANGUAGE

The USSR is home to many peoples, who speak more than 60 different languages. Russian is the official and most widely spoken language. It is written in the Cyrillic alphabet, which is a mixture of Greek and Latin letters.

АБВГДЕЁЖЗИЙКЛМНО
ПРСТУФХЦЧШЩЪЭЮЯ

Siberia is a big mining and forestry region with huge supplies of oil, coal, and wood.

The USSR's landscape varies from cool tree-less plains (tundra) and coniferous forests (taiga) to grassy plains (steppes) and deserts.

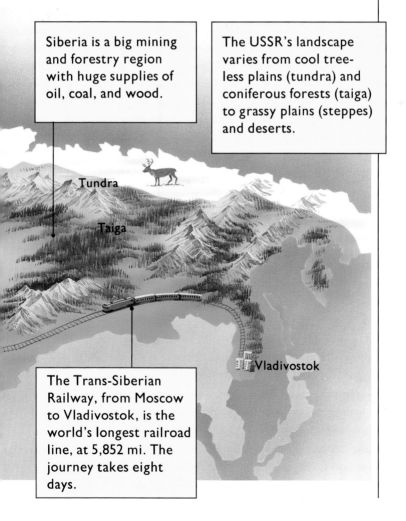

Tundra

Taiga

Vladivostok

The Trans-Siberian Railway, from Moscow to Vladivostok, is the world's longest railroad line, at 5,852 mi. The journey takes eight days.

ASIA

Asia is the world's largest continent. It is so wide that the Sun rises almost 11 hours earlier in the east than in the west.

FACT FILE

(Including the Asian part of the USSR)
Area: 17,137,820 sq mi
Independent countries: 40
Population: About 3 billion people
Largest country: The USSR*, then China
Smallest country: Republic of Maldives
Largest city: Tokyo, Japan (12 million people)
Highest mountain: Mt Everest, the Himalayas (29,029 ft)
Longest river: Chang Jiang, China (3,906 mi)

ARCTIC OCEAN

Ural Mountains

Ob

Irtysh

Ural

CASPIAN SEA

Tian

Tigris

Euphrates

Indus

Arabian Desert

RED SEA

ARABIAN SEA

INDIAN

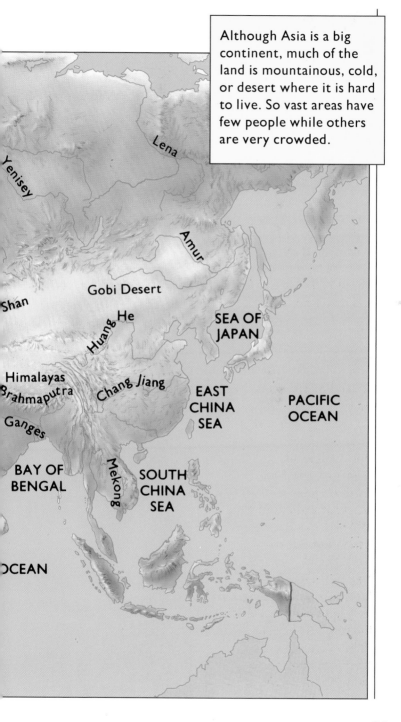

Although Asia is a big continent, much of the land is mountainous, cold, or desert where it is hard to live. So vast areas have few people while others are very crowded.

Yenisey

Lena

Amur

Shan

Gobi Desert

Huang He

Himalayas

Brahmaputra

Chang Jiang

Ganges

SEA OF JAPAN

EAST CHINA SEA

PACIFIC OCEAN

BAY OF BENGAL

Mekong

SOUTH CHINA SEA

OCEAN

Countries and Capitals

Country (Capital City)

1 USSR [part] (Moscow)
2 Mongolia (Ulan Bator)
3 Turkey (Ankara)
4 Cyprus (Nicosia)
5 Lebanon (Beirut)
6 Israel (Jerusalem)
7 Syria (Damascus)
8 Jordan (Amman)
9 Iraq (Baghdad)
10 Iran (Tehran)
11 Afghanistan (Kabul)
12 China (Beijing)
13 Korea, North (Pyongyang)
14 Korea, South (Seoul)
15 Japan (Tokyo)
16 Saudi Arabia (Riyadh)
17 Kuwait (Kuwait)
18 Bahrain (Manama)
19 Qatar (Doha)
20 United Arab Emirates (Abu Dhabi)
21 Oman (Muscat)
22 Yemen, Republic of (San'a)
23 Pakistan (Islamabad)
24 India (New Delhi)
25 Nepal (Kathmandu)
26 Bhutan (Thimbu)
27 Bangladesh (Dacca)
28 Myanmar (Yangon)
29 Laos (Vientiane)
30 Thailand (Bangkok)
31 Vietnam (Hanoi)
32 Cambodia (Phnom Penh)
33 Taiwan (Taipei)
34 Philippines (Manila)
35 Republic of Maldives (Male)
36 Sri Lanka (Colombo)
37 Malaysia (Kuala Lumpur)
38 Singapore (Singapore)
39 Brunei (Bandar Seri Begawan)
40 Indonesia (Djakarta)

ARCTIC OCEAN

RED SEA

ARABIAN SEA

INDIA

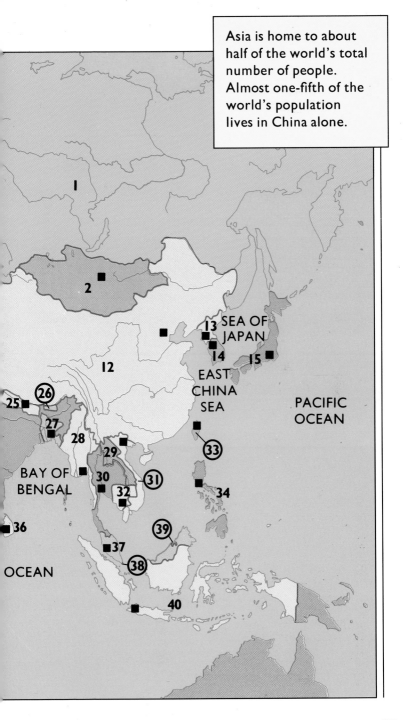

Asia is home to about half of the world's total number of people. Almost one-fifth of the world's population lives in China alone.

1

2

13

SEA OF JAPAN

14

15

12

26

25

27

28

29

30

31

32

EAST CHINA SEA

PACIFIC OCEAN

33

34

BAY OF BENGAL

36

39

37

38

OCEAN

40

Facts and Figures

Country	Population	Official Language	Currency	Flag
1 USSR*	70,000 (Total – 290,000,000)	Russian	Rouble	
2 Mongolia	2,070,000	Mongolian	Tugrik	
3 Turkey	56,740,000	Turkish	Turkish lira	
4 Cyprus	700,000	Greek, Turkish	Pound	
5 Lebanon	2,890,000	Arabic	Lebanese pound	
6 Israel	4,620,000	Hebrew, Arabic	Shekel	
7 Syria	12,000,000	Arabic	Syrian pound	
8 Jordan	4,100,000	Arabic	Jordanian dinar	
9 Iraq	18,270,000	Arabic	Iraqi dinar	
10 Iran	56,230,000	Persian (Farsi)	Rial	
11 Afghani-stan	15,810,000	Pashto, Dari	Afghani	

Country	Population	Official Language	Currency	Flag
12 China	1,160,000,000	Chinese (Mandarin)	Yuan	
13 Korea, North	22,420,000	Korean	Won	
14 Korea, South	42,930,000	Korean	Won	
15 Japan	123,120,000	Japanese	Yen	
16 Saudi Arabia	14,440,000	Arabic	Riyal	
17 Kuwait	2,050,000	Arabic	Kuwait dinar	
18 Bahrain	490,000	Arabic	Dinar	
19 Qatar	420,000	Arabic	Qatar riyal	
20 United Arab Emirates	1,550,000	Arabic	Dirham	
21 Oman	1,420,000	Arabic	Omani riyal	
22 Yemen, Republic of	11,530,000	Arabic	Dinar, Riyal	

Facts and Figures

Country	Population	Official Language	Currency	Flag
23 Pakistan	112,050,000	Urdu	Rupee	
24 India	811,820,000	Hindi, English	Rupee	
25 Nepal	18,440,000	Nepali	Rupee	
26 Bhutan	1,480,000	Dzongkha	Ngultrum	
27 Bangla-desh	106,510,000	Bengali	Taka	
28 Myanmar	40,810,000	Burmese	Kyat	
29 Laos	3,970,000	Lao	Kip	
30 Thailand	55,450,000	Thai	Baht	
31 Vietnam	65,680,000	Vietnamese	Dong	
32 Cambodia	8,060,000	Khmer	Riel	
33 Taiwan	20,260,000	Chinese (Mandarin)	Taiwan dollar	

Country	Population	Official Language	Currency	Flag
34 Philip- pines	60,100,000	English, Filipino	Peso	
35 Republic of Maldives	210,000	Divehi	Rufiyaa	
36 Sri Lanka	16,810,000	Sinhalese, Tamil	Rupee	
37 Malaysia	17,380,000	Malay	Malaysian dollar	
38 Singapore	2,700,000	Malay, Tamil Chinese, English	Singapore dollar	
39 Brunei	250,000	Malay	Brunei dollar	
40 Indonesia	180,140,000	Bahasa (Indonesian)	Rupiah	

The Great Wall of China was built over 2,000 years ago to keep out China's enemies from the north. The wall is so long that it can be seen from the Moon!

Mountains and Monsoons

Asia has three main climate regions – cool, dry, and monsoon. In the north and the mountains, the climate is cold with not much rain. Dry, desert climates are found in parts of central and southwest Asia. Southern Asia has monsoon, or warm and rainy, climates. In these regions, the summers are hot and damp and the winters are cooler and dry.

In the mountains, the climate is cold and harsh and it is hard to grow crops. People raise small herds of sheep and goats.

The Himalayas are the world's highest mountains. The lofty peaks are often called the "Roof of the World."

FLYING HIGH

Lhasa, the capital of Tibet province in China, has the world's highest airport, at 14,314 ft.

MONSOON FACTS

"Monsoon" means a season of heavy rain. Winds bring rain to the land during the summer months and there is a danger of typhoons, or severe storms. As much as 66 inches of rain can fall between June and September and only 4 inches the rest of the year.

The Philippines has over 7,000 tropical islands. Indonesia has more than 13,000!

Many island people live on boats or in wooden houses built on stilts in the water.

Rice, Rubber, and Tea

Most of the people living in Asia are farmers and fishermen. Rice grows best in hot, wet climates, so many areas in southeast Asia are good for growing it. Farmers can grow several crops a year if the rainy season is long. China produces a lot of rice, wheat, barley, cotton, and tobacco. Southeast Asia produces more rubber than any other area in the world.

RICE-GROWING

Farmers plant the rice seedlings in flooded fields. The seedlings take four or five months to grow. Then the fields are drained and the rice is harvested. In hilly areas rice is grown on special steps called terraces. Some terraces are hundreds of years old.

Thick tropical forests cover the mountains of southeast Asia. They provide woods, like mahogany and teak.

Rubber comes from the white juice, called latex, of the rubber tree. The bark of the tree is cut then the latex is drained.

Tea, coffee, and cotton are grown on plantations in cool, hilly areas. Usually, the crops are still picked by hand. India and China are famous for their many types of tea.

Oil, Carpets, and Cars

Asia's most important industrial areas are in Japan, Hong Kong, South Korea, Singapore, and Taiwan. Japan is the richest and most industrialized country in Asia. It makes metals, such as steel, and is the largest producer of cars and ships. Most of the world's oil comes from southwest Asia, from such countries as Saudi Arabia and Iran.

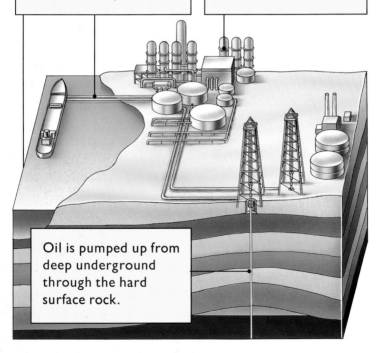

Pipelines take the oil to the coast where it is loaded onto giant oil tankers for export.

At oil refineries, oil can be changed into fuels, such as petroleum or kerosene, or chemicals.

Oil is pumped up from deep underground through the hard surface rock.

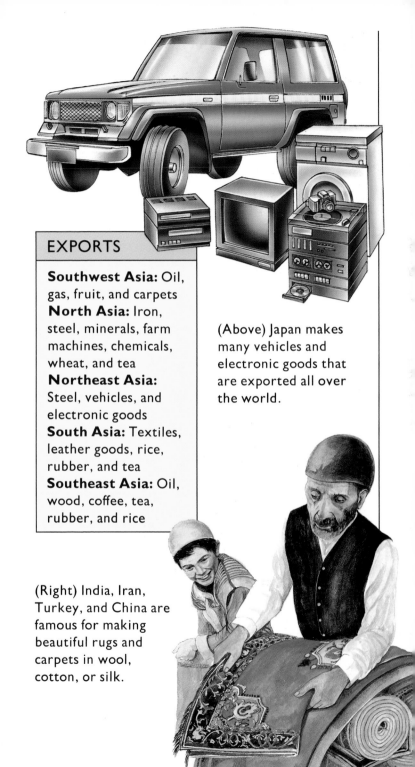

EXPORTS

Southwest Asia: Oil, gas, fruit, and carpets
North Asia: Iron, steel, minerals, farm machines, chemicals, wheat, and tea
Northeast Asia: Steel, vehicles, and electronic goods
South Asia: Textiles, leather goods, rice, rubber, and tea
Southeast Asia: Oil, wood, coffee, tea, rubber, and rice

(Above) Japan makes many vehicles and electronic goods that are exported all over the world.

(Right) India, Iran, Turkey, and China are famous for making beautiful rugs and carpets in wool, cotton, or silk.

NORTH AMERICA

North America is the world's third largest continent.

FACT FILE

Area: 9,362,539 sq mi (including Greenland, the world's biggest island)
Independent countries: 23
Population: About 420 million people
Largest country: Canada
Smallest country: St Kitts-Nevis
Largest city: New York City, USA (7.2 million people)
Highest mountain: Mt McKinley, Alaska (20,321 ft)
Longest river: Mississippi-Missouri-Red Rock, USA (3,701 mi)

ARCTIC OCEAN

Yukon

Mackenzie

Coast Mountains

Rocky Mountains

Sierra Nevada

Colorado

PACIFIC OCEAN

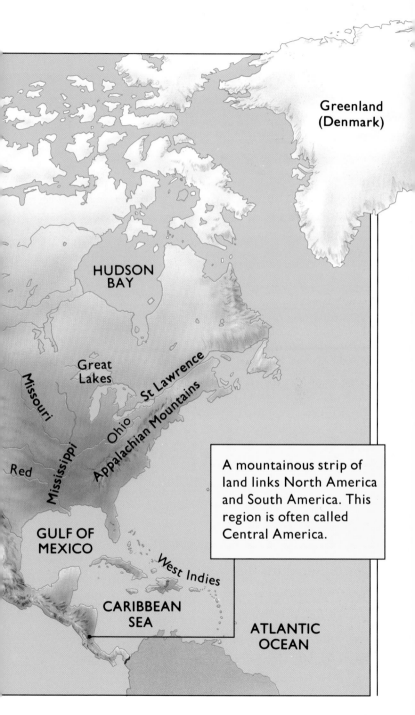

Greenland
(Denmark)

HUDSON
BAY

Great
Lakes

Missouri

Ohio

St Lawrence

Appalachian Mountains

Red

Mississippi

GULF OF
MEXICO

West Indies

CARIBBEAN
SEA

A mountainous strip of
land links North America
and South America. This
region is often called
Central America.

ATLANTIC
OCEAN

Countries and Capitals

Canada is the second largest country in the world (after the USSR). To the northwest of Canada lies Alaska, a state of the United States (see page 56).

ARCTIC OCEAN

Alaska (USA)

COUNTRIES KEY

Country (Capital City)

1 Canada (Ottawa)
2 United States (Washington, DC)
3 Mexico (Mexico City)
4 Cuba (Havana)
5 Bahamas (Nassau)
6 Haiti (Port-au-Prince)
7 Dominican Republic (Santo Domingo)
8 Belize (Belmopan)
9 Guatemala (Guatemala City)
10 El Salvador (San Salvador)
11 Honduras (Tegucigalpa)
12 Nicaragua (Managua)
13 Costa Rica (San José)
14 Panama (Panama City)
15 Jamaica (Kingston)
16 Antigua and Barbuda (St John's)
17 St Kitts-Nevis (Basseterre)
18 Dominica (Roseau)
19 St Lucia (Castries)
20 Barbados (Bridgetown)
21 St Vincent and the Grenadines (Kingstown)
22 Grenada (St George's)
23 Trinidad and Tobago (Port of Spain)

PACIFIC OCEAN

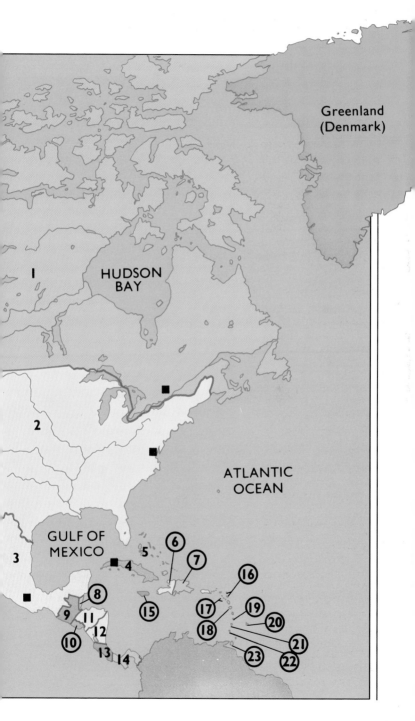

Greenland
(Denmark)

1

HUDSON
BAY

2

ATLANTIC
OCEAN

GULF OF
MEXICO

3

5   ⑥

④   ⑦   ⑯

⑧   ⑰   ⑲
⑮   ⑱   ⑳

9 11   ㉑
10 12   ㉓   ㉒
13 14

47

Facts and Figures

Country	Population	Official Language	Currency	Flag
1 Canada	26,250,000	English, French	Canadian dollar	
2 United States*	249,930,000	English	US dollar	
3 Mexico	86,150,000	Spanish	Peso	
4 Cuba	10,620,000	Spanish	Peso	
5 Bahamas	255,000	English	Bahamian dollar	
6 Haiti	5,610,000	French	Gourde	
7 Dominican Republic	7,020,000	Spanish	Peso	
8 Belize	180,000	English	Belize dollar	
9 Guatemala	9,200,000	Spanish	Quetzal	
10 El Salvador	5,210,000	Spanish	Colón	
11 Honduras	4,950,000	Spanish	Lempira	
12 Nicaragua	3,750,000	Spanish	Córdoba	

Country	Population	Official Language	Currency	Flag
13 Costa Rica	2,960,000	Spanish	Colón	
14 Panama	2,420,000	Spanish	Balboa	
15 Jamaica	2,390,000	English	Jamaican dollar	
16 Antigua and Barbuda	86,000	English	East Caribbean dollar	
17 St Kitts-Nevis	50,000	English	East Caribbean dollar	
18 Dominica	81,000	English	East Caribbean dollar	
19 St Lucia	150,000	English	East Caribbean dollar	
20 Barbados	260,000	English	Barbados dollar	
21 St Vincent and the Grenadines	110,000	English	East Caribbean dollar	
22 Grenada	100,000	English	East Caribbean dollar	
23 Trinidad and Tobago	1,260,000	English	Trinidad dollar	

*The flag of the United States is called the 'Stars and Stripes'. The first flag had 13 stars and 13 stripes to represent the original member states of America. Today, the flag has 50 stars – one for each state.

Forests and Plains

The northern part of North America sits within the icy Arctic Circle. Below is a cold and flat region with few trees. Farther south, huge forests of conifer trees stretch across the whole continent. This region is cool and snowy in winter.

Below the forests, where it is a little warmer, there are vast rolling grasslands or plains. In Canada and the United States, these grasslands are called prairies.

FOREST FACTS

Conifer trees have cones and needle-shaped leaves. Most are evergreens but some, such as larches, lose their leaves in the fall.

Pine-cones

TORNADO FACTS

Tornadoes are storms that twist and spin as hot air rises. They can cause a lot of damage because they suck up anything in their path – even cars and trains! Many tornadoes sweep across the prairies.

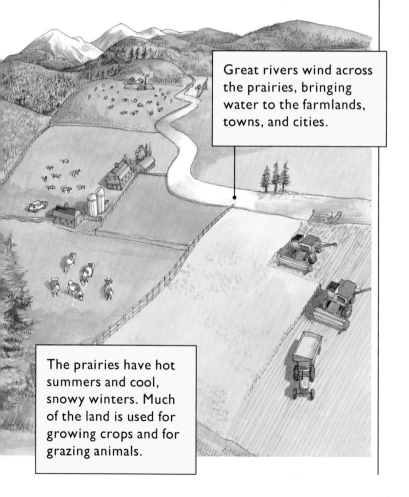

Great rivers wind across the prairies, bringing water to the farmlands, towns, and cities.

The prairies have hot summers and cool, snowy winters. Much of the land is used for growing crops and for grazing animals.

Crops, Cattle, and Fruit

North America is the greatest farming continent in the world. Its huge farms produce a lot of wheat, barley, and corn. Farmers also grow fruit and raise cattle and sheep for their meat.

In Central America, where the climate is warmer, there are many plantations growing sugar, coffee, and bananas.

BREAD BASKET OF THE WORLD

The vast farming region of southern Canada is sometimes called the "Bread Basket of the World" because it produces so much wheat, which is used to make flour for bread.

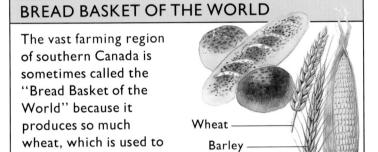

Wheat
Barley
Corn

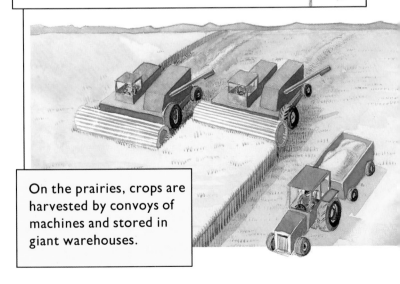

On the prairies, crops are harvested by convoys of machines and stored in giant warehouses.

Apples, cherries, and pears are grown in the cooler parts of the continent; citrus fruits and grapes are produced in the hotter areas.

In the southern parts of the United States and on many of the islands in the West Indies, farmers grow bananas, cotton, tobacco, and sugarcane.

Huge ranches in Canada and the United States raise cattle for their milk or meat.

53

Factories and Mines

North America is rich in natural gas, oil, coal, gold, copper, and iron ore. It also has uranium, which is a fuel used to make nuclear energy at power stations.

The United States has many factories. They make machines, aircraft, cars and trucks, and cloth.

Almost one-third of Canada is covered with conifer forests so Canada exports a lot of wood and makes paper for books, newspapers, and magazines.

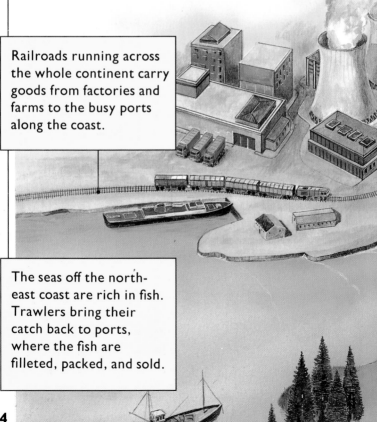

Railroads running across the whole continent carry goods from factories and farms to the busy ports along the coast.

The seas off the north-east coast are rich in fish. Trawlers bring their catch back to ports, where the fish are filleted, packed, and sold.

Power stations provide electricity for factories and homes. Power made from fast-flowing water is called hydroelectricity.

WOOD AND PAPER

Most paper comes from wood. Logs are crushed or cut into chips at paper mills then made into a squashy pulp, or paste. When dried and pressed, this makes giant sheets of paper.

55

The United States

The United States of America (USA) is the fourth largest country in the world. It is divided into 50 states including Alaska and Hawaii (see box below). The map key groups the states into different regions, such as the Pacific states and the Mid-western states.

The American bald eagle (below right) is one of the country's national symbols.

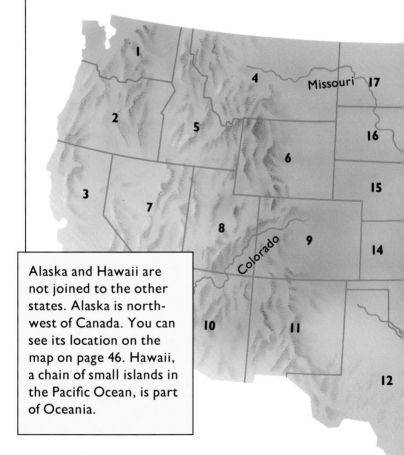

Alaska and Hawaii are not joined to the other states. Alaska is north-west of Canada. You can see its location on the map on page 46. Hawaii, a chain of small islands in the Pacific Ocean, is part of Oceania.

THE STATES OF THE USA

(Pacific Coast)
1 Washington
2 Oregon
3 California

(Rocky Mountain)
4 Montana
5 Idaho
6 Wyoming
7 Nevada
8 Utah
9 Colorado

(South-western)
10 Arizona
11 New Mexico
12 Texas
13 Oklahoma

(Mid-western)
14 Kansas
15 Nebraska

16 South Dakota
17 North Dakota
18 Minnesota
19 Iowa
20 Wisconsin
21 Michigan
22 Ohio
23 Indiana
24 Illinois
25 Missouri

(Southern)
26 Arkansas
27 Louisiana
28 Mississippi
29 Alabama
30 Florida
31 Georgia
32 South Carolina
33 North Carolina

34 Tennessee
35 Kentucky
36 Virginia
37 West Virginia
38 Maryland
39 Delaware

(Mid-Atlantic)
40 New Jersey
41 Pennsylvania
42 New York

(New England)
43 Connecticut
44 Rhode Island
45 Massachusetts
46 New Hampshire
47 Vermont
48 Maine
49 Alaska
50 Hawaii

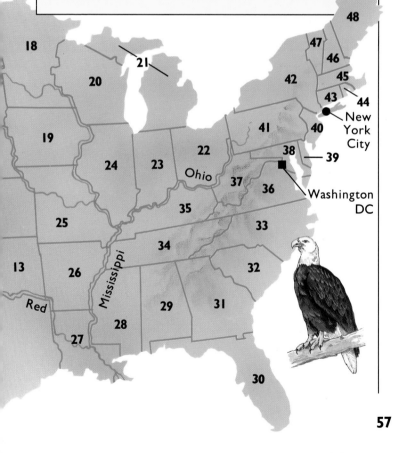

New York City

Washington DC

Ohio

Mississippi

Red

SOUTH AMERICA

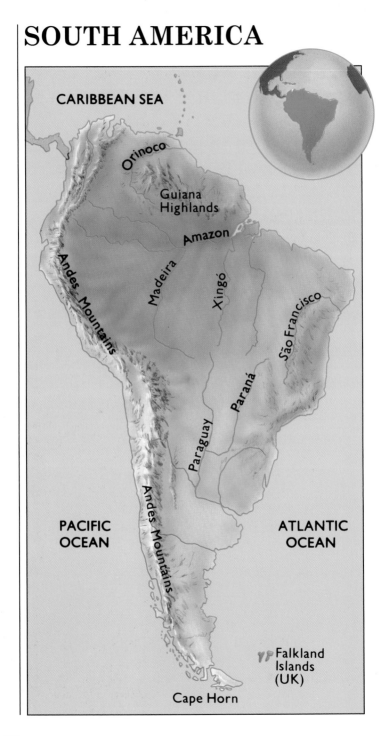

CARIBBEAN SEA

Orinoco

Guiana Highlands

Amazon

Madeira

Xingó

São Francisco

Andes Mountains

Paraná

Paraguay

Andes Mountains

PACIFIC OCEAN

ATLANTIC OCEAN

Falkland Islands (UK)

Cape Horn

South America is the world's fourth largest continent. Most of the continent is hot, but the mountains and the far south are cool for most of the year.

The Atacama Desert in the north of Chile is the Earth's driest region. Some parts had no rain for 400 years until a freak storm occurred in 1971. The world's wettest place is also in South America, in Tutunendo, Colombia. It usually has 430 inches of rain a year.

FACT FILE

Area: 6,795,360 sq mi
Independent countries: 12
Population: About 290 million people
Largest country: Brazil
Smallest country: French Guiana, then Suriname
Largest city: Buenos Aires, Argentina (10.8 million people)
Highest mountain: Mt. Aconcagua, Andes Mountains (22,835 ft)
Longest river: Amazon (3,991 mi)

Tutunendo

Atacama Desert

Countries and Capitals

Large parts of South America contain high mountains or dense rain forests where it is difficult for people to live. Most towns and cities are near the coast where the land is flatter and can be farmed more easily.

Many South Americans are descendants of Spanish and Portuguese explorers who came to South America in the 1500s looking for gold and riches.

The Incas were people who lived in South America hundreds of years ago. They ruled a large empire. You can still see the ruins of some of their cities high in the Andes Mountains.

COUNTRIES KEY

Country (Capital City)

1. Venezuela (Caracas)
2. Colombia (Bogotá)
3. Guyana (Georgetown)
4. Suriname (Paramaribo)
5. French Guiana [France] (Cayenne)
6. Ecuador (Quito)
7. Peru (Lima)
8. Brazil (Brasília)
9. Bolivia (La Paz)
10. Paraguay (Asunción)
11. Chile (Santiago)
12. Argentina (Buenos Aires)
13. Uruguay (Montevideo)

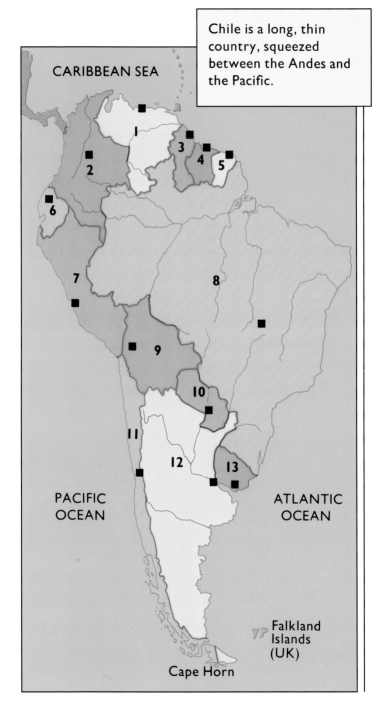

CARIBBEAN SEA

Chile is a long, thin country, squeezed between the Andes and the Pacific.

1

2

3

4

5

6

7

8

9

10

11

12

13

PACIFIC OCEAN

ATLANTIC OCEAN

Falkland Islands (UK)

Cape Horn

Facts and Figures

Country	Population	Official Language	Currency	Flag
1 Venezuela	19,250,000	Spanish	Bolivar	
2 Colombia	31,190,000	Spanish	Peso	
3 Guyana	1,020,000	English	Guyanese dollar	
4 Suriname	400,000	Dutch	Guilder	
5 French Guiana (France)	90,000	French	French franc	
6 Ecuador	10,500,000	Spanish	Sucre	
7 Peru	22,790,000	Spanish	Inti	
8 Brazil	150,370,000	Portuguese	Cruzado	
9 Bolivia	7,190,000	Spanish	Boliviano	

Country	Population	Official Language	Currency	Flag
10 Paraguay	4,160,000	Spanish	Guarani	
11 Chile	12,960,000	Spanish	Peso	
12 Argentina	32,320,000	Spanish	Austral	
13 Uruguay	3,070,000	Spanish	Peso	

Lake Titicaca, on the borders of Peru and Bolivia, is the world's highest navigable lake. Reeds growing around the shores are used to make fishing boats.

Rain Forests

Surrounding the mighty rivers in the northeast of South America is the largest area of tropical forest, or rain forest, in the world. It is almost as big as the whole of Australia. Rain forests grow near the Equator where it is hot all year round. There are rainstorms nearly every day and the air is humid, or damp. Thousands of kinds of animals, particularly birds and insects, live in the forests. Most live in the upper layers, where there is more sunlight.

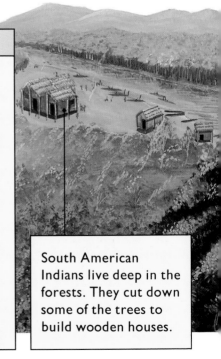

FOREST FACTS

• Rain forest plants are used to make some of our medicines. The first aspirin, for example, came from tree bark.

• South American rain forests contain more than 150,000 types of insects.

• Lianas, or ropelike plants, hang down from the canopy layer. Most are thick and strong enough to swing on!

South American Indians live deep in the forests. They cut down some of the trees to build wooden houses.

The tallest trees in the rain forests grow to 165 ft or more. They form the attic layer.

The canopy layer, at 100 ft, is a thick mass of tree tops blocking out the sunlight.

In the lower layers, where it is dark and damp, young trees struggle to grow toward the light.

Mountains and Pampas

South America has a varied climate, so farmers can grow a wide range of crops and fruit. Sugarcane and bananas are grown on the flatter, warmer lands. Higher in the mountains, where it is cooler, wheat and beans are grown. On the flat temperate grasslands, called "pampas," there are huge cattle ranches like the ones in North America.

People living high in the Andes Mountains tend herds of llamas for their milk, meat, and hides, and grow vegetables to sell at local markets.

FARMING FACTS

- Brazil is the world's largest producer of sugarcane. Some cars in Brazil are powered by a fuel made from sugarcane, called "gasahol."

- In South America, a type of large guinea pig is raised on farms to eat as meat.

- Argentina is the world's third largest producer of beef.

Coffee is a major crop in Colombia, Brazil, and Ecuador. The coffee beans are exported all over the world.

On the pampas, cattle are rounded up by cowboys on horseback. In South America cowboys are called "gauchos."

Oil, Copper, and Gold

In South America, Venezuela and Brazil have the most natural resources and the most industries. Venezuela has oil, iron ore, and gold. It is the continent's richest country. Brazil has no oil but it has lots of coal and iron ore. It gets most of its electricity from the Itaipu Dam on the Paraná River. This forms the largest hydroelectric power system in the world.

Boats dredge the streams and riverbeds to find rocks bearing gold and other precious metals.

Rigs pump oil from huge reserves that lie beneath the sea and under the beds of lakes.

Some places in the Andes Mountains are rich in precious stones, minerals, and metals. So mining is important in most of the Andean countries. For example, Chile's main export is copper and Peru exports silver, lead, and zinc.

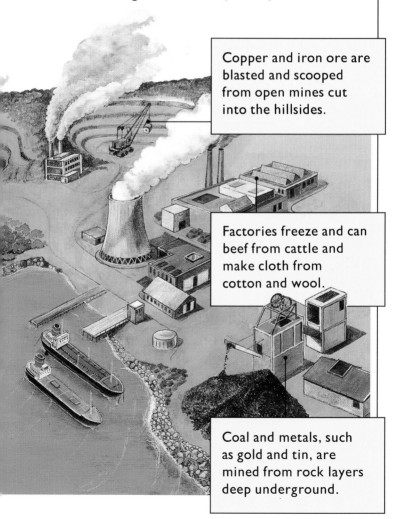

Copper and iron ore are blasted and scooped from open mines cut into the hillsides.

Factories freeze and can beef from cattle and make cloth from cotton and wool.

Coal and metals, such as gold and tin, are mined from rock layers deep underground.

AFRICA

Africa, the second largest continent in the world, is nearly three times as big as Europe. Most of Africa is a plateau, or a high and flat plain. Unlike other continents it has no major mountain ranges.

FACT FILE

Area: 11,706,165 sq mi
Independent countries: 52
Population: About 650 million people
Largest country: Sudan
Smallest country: Seychelles (islands in the Indian Ocean)
Largest city: Cairo, Egypt (6 million people)
Highest mountain: Mt Kilimanjaro (19,340 ft)
Longest river: Nile (4,135 mi)

Atlas Mountains

Niger

ATLANTIC OCEAN

Thick rain forests cover the central regions, near the Equator. To the north and south of the forests are grasslands called savannas.

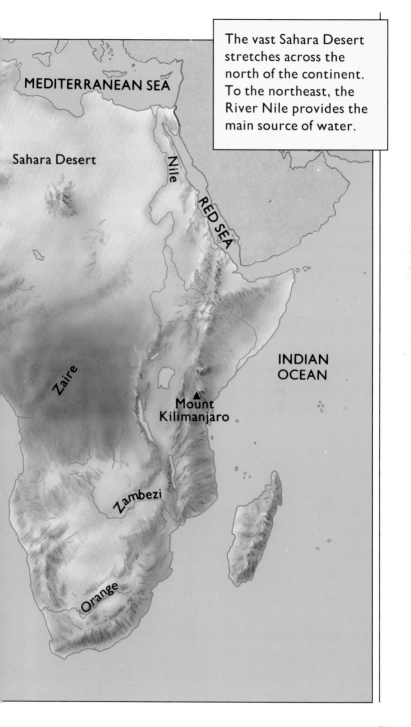

MEDITERRANEAN SEA

Sahara Desert

Nile

RED SEA

The vast Sahara Desert stretches across the north of the continent. To the northeast, the River Nile provides the main source of water.

INDIAN OCEAN

Zaire

▲
Mount Kilimanjaro

Zambezi

Orange

Countries and Capitals

Country (Capital City)

1 Morocco (Rabat)
2 Algeria (Algiers)
3 Tunisia (Tunis)
4 Libya (Tripoli)
5 Egypt (Cairo)
6 Cape Verde (Praia)
7 Mauritania (Nouakchott)
8 Mali (Bamako)
9 Niger (Niamey)
10 Chad (N'Djamena)
11 Sudan (Khartoum)
12 Senegal (Dakar)
13 Gambia (Banjul)
14 Guinea-Bissau (Bissau)
15 Guinea (Conakry)
16 Sierra Leone (Freetown)
17 Liberia (Monrovia)
18 Burkina Faso
   (Ouagadougou)
19 Ivory Coast (Abidjan)
20 Ghana (Accra)
21 Togo (Lomé)
22 Benin (Porto-Novo)
23 Nigeria (Lagos)
24 Central African Republic
   (Bangui)
25 Djibouti (Jibuti)
26 Ethiopia (Addis Ababa)
27 Somalia (Mogadishu)
28 São Tomé and Príncipe
   (São Tomé)
29 Equatorial Guinea
   (Malabo)
30 Cameroon (Yaoundé)
31 Gabon (Libreville)
32 Congo (Brazzaville)
33 Zaire (Kinshasa)
34 Rwanda (Kigali)
35 Burundi (Bujumbura)
36 Uganda (Kampala)
37 Kenya (Nairobi)
38 Tanzania (Dar es Salaam)
39 Seychelles (Victoria)
40 Angola (Luanda)

41 Zambia (Lusaka)
42 Malawi (Lilongwe)
43 Comoro Islands (Moroni)
44 South-West Africa
   (Windhoek)
45 Botswana (Gaborone)
46 Zimbabwe (Harare)
47 Mozambique (Maputo)
48 Madagascar
   (Antananarivo)
49 Mauritius (Port Louis)
50 South Africa (Pretoria,
   Cape Town, and
   Bloemfontein)
51 Lesotho (Maseru)
52 Swaziland (Mbabane)

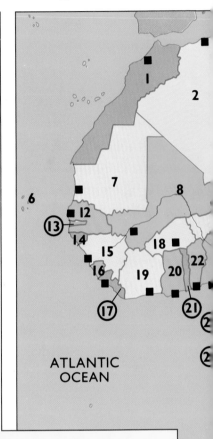

ATLANTIC
OCEAN

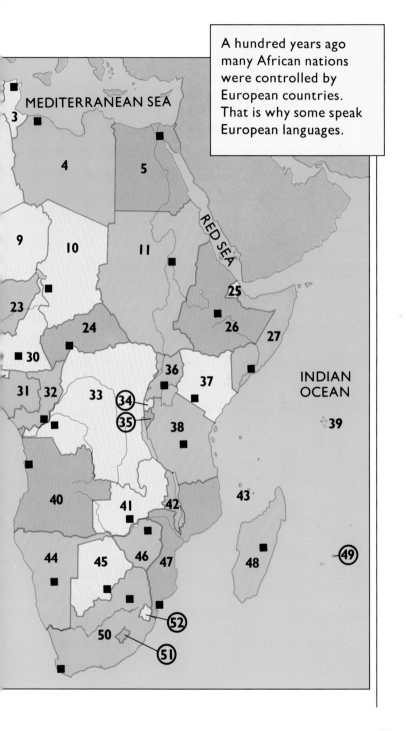

MEDITERRANEAN SEA

RED SEA

INDIAN OCEAN

A hundred years ago many African nations were controlled by European countries. That is why some speak European languages.

3
4
5
9
10
11
23
24
25
26
27
30
31
32
33
34
35
36
37
38
39
40
41
42
43
44
45
46
47
48
49
50
51
52

Facts and Figures

Country	Population	Official Language	Currency	Flag
1 Morocco	24,520,000	Arabic	Dirham	
2 Algeria	24,600,000	Arabic	Algerian dinar	
3 Tunisia	7,990,000	Arabic	Tunisian dinar	
4 Libya	4,380,000	Arabic	Libyan dinar	
5 Egypt	51,730,000	Arabic	Egyptian pound	
6 Cape Verde	370,000	Portuguese	Escudo	
7 Mauritania	1,970,000	Arabic, French	Ouguiya	
8 Mali	7,960,000	French	Franc CFA	
9 Niger	7,250,000	French	Franc CFA	
10 Chad	5,540,000	French	Franc CFA	
11 Sudan	24,490,000	Arabic	Sudanese pound	
12 Senegal	7,170,000	French	Franc CFA	
13 Gambia	840,000	English	Dalasi	

Country	Population	Official Language	Currency	Flag
14 Guinea-Bissau	970,000	Portuguese	Peso	
15 Guinea	6,710,000	French	Guinea franc	
16 Sierra Leone	4,050,000	English	Leone	
17 Liberia	2,510,000	English	Liberian dollar	
18 Burkina Faso	9,000,000	French	Franc CFA	
19 Ivory Coast	12,100,000	French	Franc CFA	
20 Ghana	14,570,000	English	Cedi	
21 Togo	3,350,000	French	Franc CFA	
22 Benin	4,590,000	French	Franc CFA	
23 Nigeria	109,170,000	English	Naira	
24 Central African Republic	2,840,000	French	Franc CFA	
25 Djibouti	400,000	French	Djibouti franc	
26 Ethiopia	50,770,000	Amharic	Birr	

Facts and Figures

Country	Population	Official Language	Currency	Flag
27 Somalia	7,340,000	Somali	Somali shilling	
28 São Tomé & Principe	120,000	Portuguese	Dobra	
29 Equatorial Guinea	340,000	Spanish	Franc CFA	
30 Cameroon	11,540,000	English, French	Franc CFA	
31 Gabon	1,200,000	French	Franc CFA	
32 Congo	1,940,000	French	Franc CFA	
33 Zaire	34,490,000	French	Zaire	
34 Rwanda	6,990,000	French, Kinyarwanda	Rwanda franc	
35 Burundi	5,300,000	French, Kirundi	Burundi franc	
36 Uganda	17,800,000	English	Ugandan shilling	
37 Kenya	24,870,000	English, Swahili	Kenya shilling	
38 Tanzania	24,400,000	English, Swahili	Tanzanian shilling	
39 Seychelles	67,000	English, French	Rupee	

Country	Population	Official Language	Currency	Flag
40 Angola	9,750,000	Portuguese	Kwanza	
41 Zambia	8,070,000	English	Kwacha	
42 Malawi	8,020,000	English, Chichewa	Kwacha	
43 Comoro Islands	500,000	French	Franc CFA	
44 South-West Africa	1,820,000	Afrikaans, English	Rand	
45 Botswana	1,260,000	English, Setswana	Pula	
46 Zim-babwe	9,120,000	English	Zimbabwe dollar	
47 Mozam-bique	15,330,000	Portuguese	Metical	
48 Mada-gascar	11,600,000	French, Malagasy	Malgache franc	
49 Mauritius	1,070,000	English	Rupee	
50 South Africa	34,490,000	Afrikaans, English	Rand	
51 Lesotho	1,700,000	English, Sesotho	Loti	
52 Swaziland	760,000	English, Swazi	Lilangeni	

Deserts and Grasslands

The whole of Africa is hot, except near the tops of high mountains, but rainfall varies greatly. The Sahara Desert in the north gets little rain, so much of the land is a wasteland where almost nothing can grow. Some areas near the Equator have heavy rainfall and are covered with tropical forests. The savanna grasslands have a long dry season and a short rainy season. They are home to the world's largest herds of animals.

Camels can go for days without water. They are used to carry goods and people in desert areas.

In the hot and dry desert regions people live close to water holes called oases.

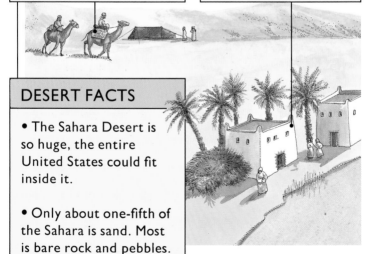

DESERT FACTS

• The Sahara Desert is so huge, the entire United States could fit inside it.

• Only about one-fifth of the Sahara is sand. Most is bare rock and pebbles.

SAVANNA GRASSLANDS

Great herds of zebras, elephants, antelopes, and giraffes roam the vast savanna lands in eastern Africa, feeding on the tall grasses and thorny bushes. Today, many of Africa's wild animals are protected in game reserves.

(Right) In the wetter regions that were once covered with tropical rain forests, people are able to grow coffee, rubber, and cocoa, which comes from the seeds of the cacao tree.

(Left) On the dry, dusty plains, farmers struggle to grow crops like millet and sorghum. Many, like the Masai people, raise cattle.

Fishing and Mining

Most African people are farmers or fishermen, but industry is growing fast. Oil and oil products are major exports in northern Africa. Western Africa is rich in oil, iron ore, and diamonds. South Africa has plenty of minerals and is the biggest producer of gold in the world. It also mines diamonds, which are found in volcanic rocks, and coal.

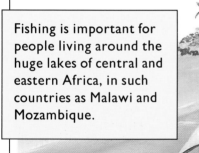

Fishing is important for people living around the huge lakes of central and eastern Africa, in such countries as Malawi and Mozambique.

Many ships transport goods along the Suez Canal, which links the Mediterranean Sea and the Red Sea through northeast Egypt.

BIG DIAMOND

The world's largest uncut diamond, the "Cullinan," was found in South Africa in 1905. It was as big as a grapefruit and weighed over a pound.

MINING FACTS

• Almost half the world's gold is mined in South Africa alone.

• The Western Deep gold mine in South Africa is the deepest mine in the world, at about 12,370 ft.

• The world's oldest known mines are in Swaziland. People mined iron there about 43,000 years ago.

Rubble taken from the rock face is crushed so that the gold can be separated out.

Miners drill deep holes in the rock face. The holes are then packed with explosives to blow the rock apart.

OCEANIA

South and east of Asia lie thousands of tiny islands dotted across the Pacific Ocean. With the countries of Australia and New Zealand, these islands form a region called Oceania. Australia is the world's smallest continent.

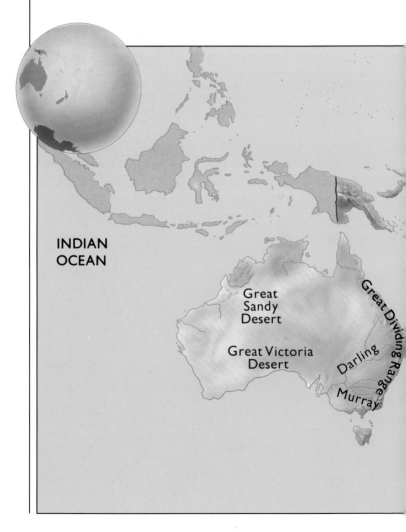

INDIAN
OCEAN

Great
Sandy
Desert

Great Victoria
Desert

Great Dividing Range

Darling

Murray

Hundreds of the Pacific islands are volcanoes or bare, flat stretches of coral. Many have no people living on them.

FACT FILE

Area: 3,285,700 sq mi
Independent countries: 11
Population: About 26 million people
Largest country: Australia
Smallest country: Nauru
Largest city: Sydney, Australia (3.5 million people)
Highest mountain: Mt Wilhelm, Papua New Guinea (15,400 ft)
Longest river: Murray (1,600 mi); Darling (1,700 ft) doesn't flow all year.

PACIFIC OCEAN

CORAL SEA

TASMAN SEA

New Zealand has two main islands. North Island is famous for its many geysers, hot springs, boiling mud pools, and volcanoes.

Countries and Capitals

Most of the island nations in the Pacific Ocean are not independent countries. For example, French Polynesia is controlled by France, and Hawaii is a state of the United States. This map names only the independent countries.

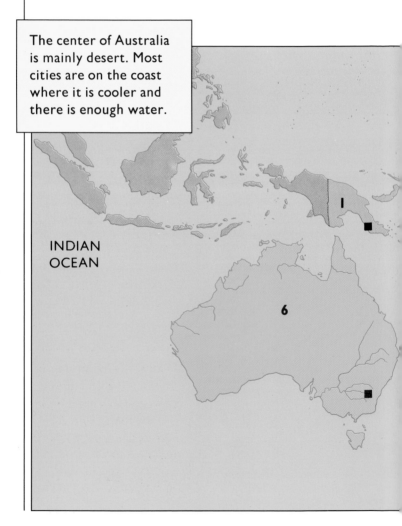

The center of Australia is mainly desert. Most cities are on the coast where it is cooler and there is enough water.

INDIAN OCEAN

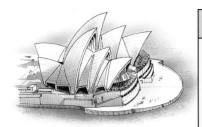

The roof of the Opera House in Sydney looks like the sails of a ship. Sydney is Australia's largest city.

COUNTRIES KEY

Country (Capital City)

1 Papua New Guinea (Port Moresby)
2 Solomon Islands (Honiara)
3 Nauru (–)
4 Kiribati (Tarawa)
5 Tuvalu (Funafuti)
6 Australia (Canberra)
7 Vanuatu (Port Vila)
8 Fiji (Suva)
9 Western Samoa (Apia)
10 Tonga (Nukualofa)
11 New Zealand (Wellington)

3

4

2

5   PACIFIC OCEAN

CORAL
SEA   7   8   9

10

TASMAN
SEA

11

Most of the countries in Oceania are groups of tiny islands. Papua New Guinea has over 600 islands and Tonga has around 160.

Facts and Figures

Country	Population	Official Language	Currency	Flag
1 Papua New Guinea	3,590,000	English	Kina	
2 Solomon Islands	320,000	English	Soloman Islands dollar	
3 Nauru	9,000	English, Nauruan	Australian dollar	
4 Kiribati	70,000	English	Australian dollar	
5 Tuvalu	9,000	English, Tuvaluan	Australian dollar	
6 Australia	17,030,000	English	Australian dollar	
7 Vanuatu	155,000	Bislama, English, French	Vatu	
8 Fiji	727,000	English	Fiji dollar	
9 Western Samoa	160,000	English, Samoan	Tala	

Country	Population	Official Language	Currency	Flag
10 Tonga	100,000	English, Tongan	Pa'anga	
11 New Zealand	3,370,000	English	New Zealand dollar	

Animals like the koala, the wallaby, and the kangaroo are found only in Australia. They are called marsupials — animals that rear their young in pouches.

The white flesh found inside the fruit of the coconut palm can be eaten or used in making soap, wax, and oil.

The boomerang is a wooden throwing stick used mostly by the Aborigines, the native people of Australia. Some boomerangs are shaped in a special way so that they will return to the thrower.

Deserts and Islands

The Pacific is the world's largest ocean, and distances between land areas are vast. Australia is mainly a hot and dry desert, but New Zealand, much farther to the southeast, has a temperate climate. In the southern part of the world, the seasons are the opposite of those in the north. So when it is summer in Europe, it is winter in Australia.

The huge desert areas of Australia are often called the Outback or the "dead heart" of the country.

STONE PEOPLE

Ancient stone statues stand on Easter Island. These huge carvings were made with simple stone axes by people who once lived there but then moved away.

ISLAND FACTS

• The name Tonga means "Friendly Islands."

• No one knows just how many islands are in the Pacific Ocean. There may be 30,000 or more.

• Papua New Guinea shares its biggest island with the Asian country of Indonesia.

People of the smaller Pacific islands live mainly in villages. They grow their own crops, such as coconuts, pine-apples, and bananas, and fish from wooden boats and canoes.

Sheep and Cattle

Raising sheep and cattle is the major type of farming in Australia and New Zealand. Both countries export a lot of wool, lamb, and beef and produce dairy foods, like milk, butter, and cheese. They also grow wheat, fruit, and vegetables. On the smaller islands, the main crop is copra, or dried coconut.

Animals fed on the rich grass of New Zealand's farms produce excellent meat and milk.

FARMING FACTS

• In Australia and New Zealand, sheep and cattle outnumber people by more than ten to one!

• Some of the sheep and cattle stations in Australia are as big as the state of Vermont in the United States.

Metals and Wood

Australia and New Zealand have plenty of coal. Australia also has oil and lots of metals, such as gold, silver, copper, and lead. It is the world's sixth largest producer of gold. Both New Zealand and Papua New Guinea export wood from the thick forests growing on their cool mountain slopes.

In mountain areas, water is channelled through hydro-electric power stations to produce electricity.

People living in remote areas in central parts of Australia rely on aircraft for food and supplies.

Huge trucks are used to carry goods across the Australian Outback.

USEFUL WORDS

Canal   Channel or river built to carry cargo boats, barges, and ships. Some canals are used to irrigate, or water, dry land. In low-lying countries, such as the Netherlands, they are used to drain the land.

Cocoa   Comes from the pods of the cacao tree which is grown in western Africa, the Caribbean, and South America. The beans are dried, roasted, and ground until a brown liquid forms. This is used to make cocoa powder and chocolate.

Equator   An imaginary line going round the Earth's middle. The Sun's heat is most intense at the Equator, so it is hotter there.

Exports   Goods that are sold to another country.

Fjord   A steep-sided narrow coastal valley that has been worn away by ice and where the sea has invaded the land. Fjords are found in Greenland, New Zealand, and Norway.

Geyser   A hot spring that squirts out steam and boiling water from deep cracks under the ground. Most geysers are found in Iceland, New Zealand, and the United States.

Marsupial   An animal with a pouch in which it rears its young. A newly born marsupial is very tiny. It crawls into its mother's pouch and feeds on her milk until it is old enough to look after itself. Most marsupials live in Australia. They include the koala, kangaroos, and wallabies.

Mineral Any natural material found in the ground that does not come from a plant or an animal. All rocks are made up of minerals.

Oasis Area in a desert with water at or near the surface of the ground. At oases, people get water from springs or wells and so can farm the land.

Plantation A large farm on which one crop is usually grown. Often the first stage of processing takes place there. For example, on a tea plantation the tea leaves are dried and crushed.

Savanna Tropical grassland where it is hot all year. Savanna grassland has two seasons. In the wet season the tall savanna grass is green and lush. In the dry season it is brown and dry. Savanna grassland is found in Africa.

Sorghum Tropical grass grown for grain and hay.

Resources The Earth's resources include the air, the water, and the land and its minerals.

Tropics Lines of latitude circling the globe. They mark where the Sun is directly overhead on midsummer's day. On June 21 the Sun is directly overhead at the Tropic of Cancer. On December 21 it is overhead at the Tropic of Capricorn. The hot tropical lands lie between the Tropics.

Volcano An opening in the Earth's surface from which gas, hot liquid rock, and ash escape.

INDEX OF COUNTRIES

Bold numbers are for maps.